CURSIVE HANDWRITING WORKBOOK FOR KIDS

BEGINNING CURSIVE

Welcome to Brighter Child's *Cursive Handwriting Workbook For Kids*. This workbook has been specifically designed to take your child from the very beginning of their cursive journey to the stage where they are confidently writing words.

The workbook uses Brighter Child's unique 'dot to dot' illustrated exercise system so kids can easily trace the letters and learn the correct sequence in which to perform their pencil strokes. This ensures they form the correct writing habits from the earliest stage to write well-formed letters and words.

HOW THIS WORKBOOK IS STRUCTURED

This workbook is split into the following parts.

Part: 1 The alphabet
Learn to write every letter of the alphabet - uppercase and lowercase - until each one has been perfected. Use the dot to dot method for easy learning.

Part 2: Joining letters
Here we learn how to connect cursive letters together in preparation for writing words.

Part 3: Writing words
Now we use all the skills we have learnt so far to write a selection of words. We start easy and work up to more complex words.

Part 4: Practice paper
Ruled writing paper pages are provided to further practise cursive handwriting on your own, or re-try any words that were particularly tricky.

Part 1: Learning The Cursive Alphabet

a b c d e f g h i j k l m n o p q r s t u v w x y z

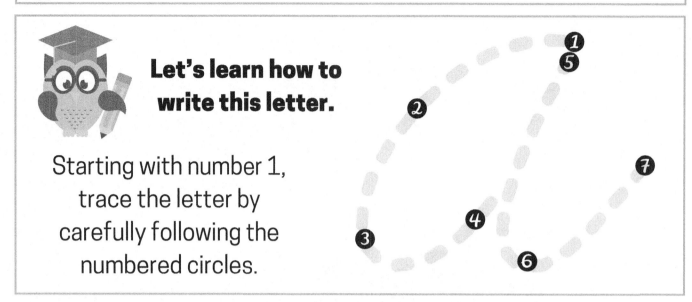

Let's learn how to write this letter.

Starting with number 1, trace the letter by carefully following the numbered circles.

Now let's practice! Trace the letters using the example above.

a a a a a a a a a a

a a a a a a a a a a

a a a a a a a a a a

Your turn! Write the letter on your own.

a

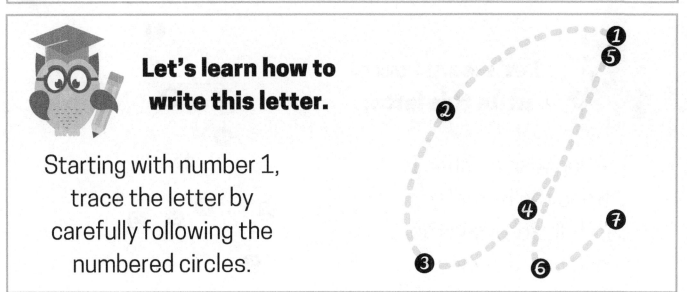

Let's learn how to write this letter.

Starting with number 1, trace the letter by carefully following the numbered circles.

Now let's practice! Trace the letters using the example above.

a a a a a a a a

a a a a a a a a

a a a a a a a a

Your turn! Write the letter on your own.

a

a **b** *c d e f g h i j k l m n o p q r s t u v w x y z*

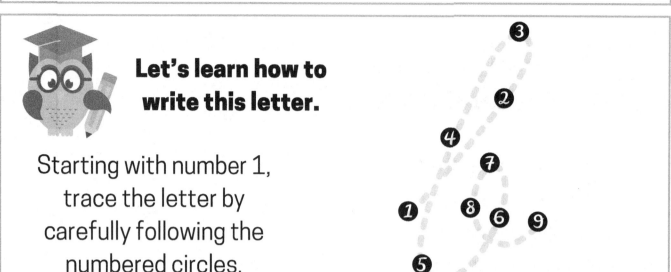

Let's learn how to write this letter.

Starting with number 1, trace the letter by carefully following the numbered circles.

Now let's practice! Trace the letters using the example above.

Your turn! Write the letter on your own.

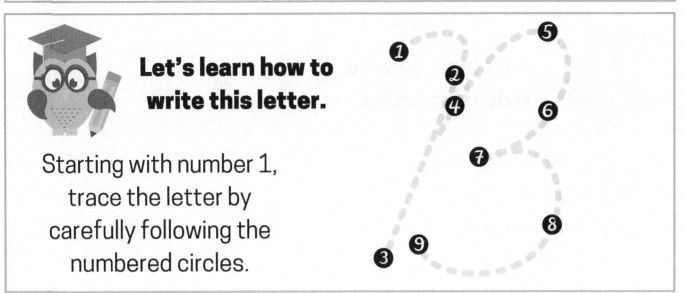

a B C D E F G H I J K L M N O P Q R S T U V W X Y Z

Let's learn how to write this letter.

Starting with number 1, trace the letter by carefully following the numbered circles.

Now let's practice! Trace the letters using the example above.

B B B B B B B B B

B B B B B B B B B

B B B B B B B B B

Your turn! Write the letter on your own.

B

a b **c** *d e f g h i j k l m n o p q r s t u v w x y z*

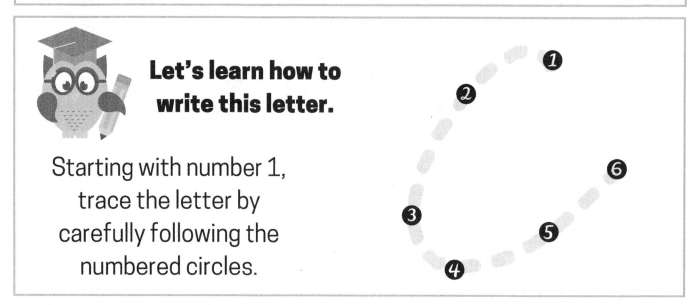

Let's learn how to write this letter.

Starting with number 1, trace the letter by carefully following the numbered circles.

Now let's practice! Trace the letters using the example above.

c c c c c c c c c c c c

c c c c c c c c c c c c

c c c c c c c c c c c c

Your turn! Write the letter on your own.

C

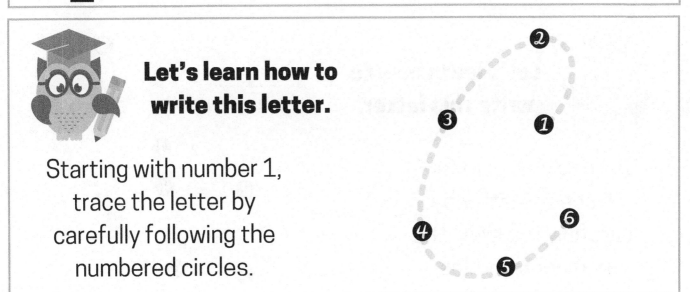

a B C D E F G H I J K L M N O P Q R S T U V W X Y Z

Let's learn how to write this letter.

Starting with number 1, trace the letter by carefully following the numbered circles.

Now let's practice! Trace the letters using the example above.

C C C C C C C C C C

C C C C C C C C C C

C C C C C C C C C C

Your turn! Write the letter on your own.

C

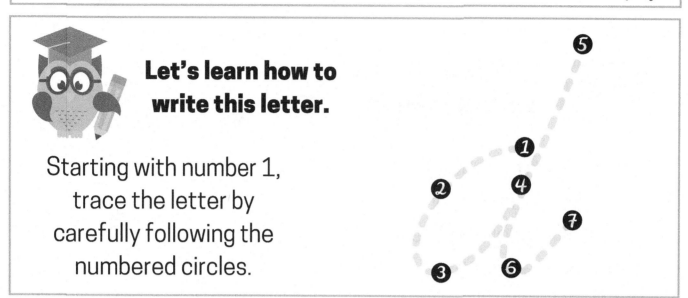

Starting with number 1, trace the letter by carefully following the numbered circles.

Now let's practice! Trace the letters using the example above.

d d d d d d d d d

d d d d d d d d d

d d d d d d d d d

Your turn! Write the letter on your own.

d

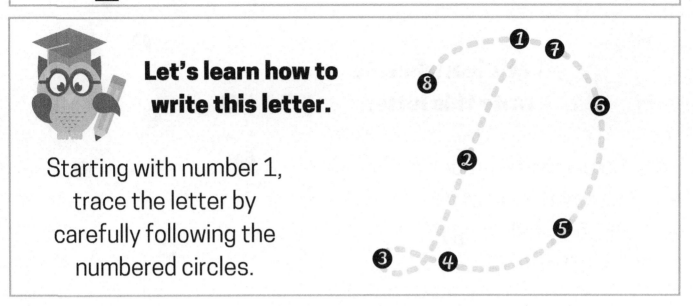

Starting with number 1, trace the letter by carefully following the numbered circles.

Now let's practice! Trace the letters using the example above.

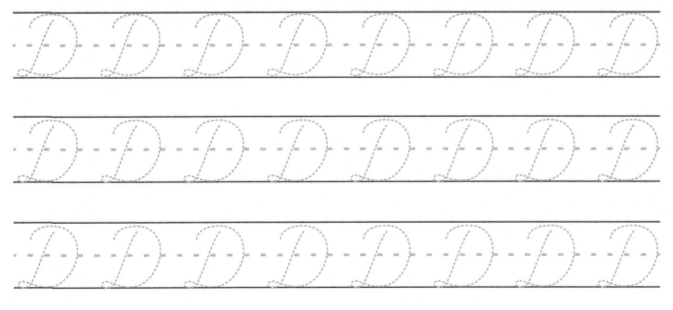

Your turn! Write the letter on your own.

D

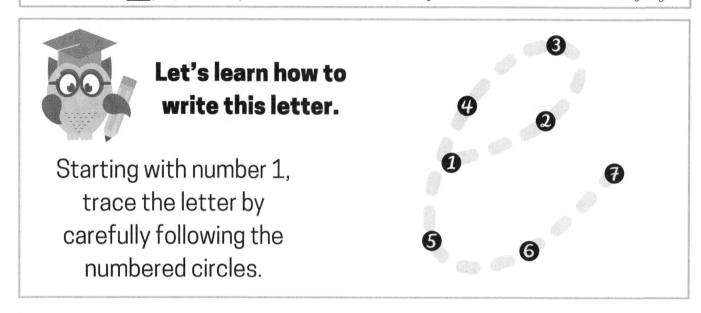

a b c d e f g h i j k l m n o p q r s t u v w x y z

Let's learn how to write this letter.

Starting with number 1, trace the letter by carefully following the numbered circles.

Now let's practice! Trace the letters using the example above.

e e e e e e e e e e e e e

e e e e e e e e e e e e e

e e e e e e e e e e e e e

Your turn! Write the letter on your own.

e

Starting with number 1, trace the letter by carefully following the numbered circles.

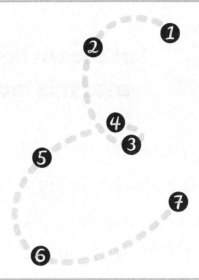

Now let's practice! Trace the letters using the example above.

Your turn! Write the letter on your own.

a b c d e **f** *g h i j k l m n o p q r s t u v w x y z*

Let's learn how to write this letter.

Starting with number 1, trace the letter by carefully following the numbered circles.

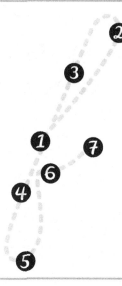

Now let's practice! Trace the letters using the example above.

Your turn! Write the letter on your own.

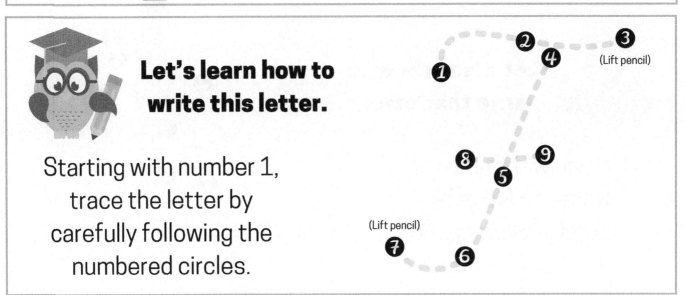

Let's learn how to write this letter.

Starting with number 1, trace the letter by carefully following the numbered circles.

① ② ③ (Lift pencil)
④
⑧ ⑨
⑤
(Lift pencil)
⑦ ⑥

Now let's practice! Trace the letters using the example above.

Your turn! Write the letter on your own.

a b c d e f g h i j k l m n o p q r s t u v w x y z

Let's learn how to write this letter.

Starting with number 1, trace the letter by carefully following the numbered circles.

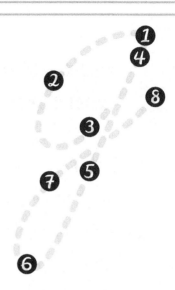

Now let's practice! Trace the letters using the example above.

Your turn! Write the letter on your own.

A B C D E F G H I J K L M N O P Q R S T U V W X Y Z

Let's learn how to write this letter.

Starting with number 1, trace the letter by carefully following the numbered circles.

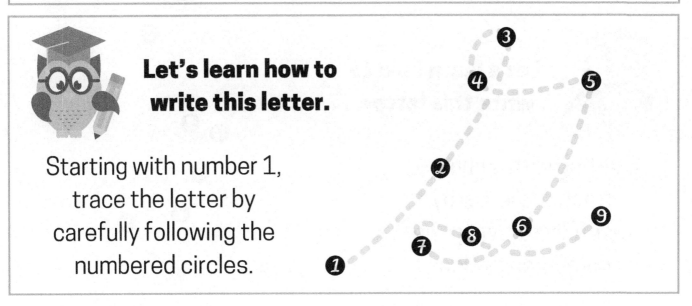

Now let's practice! Trace the letters using the example above.

Your turn! Write the letter on your own.

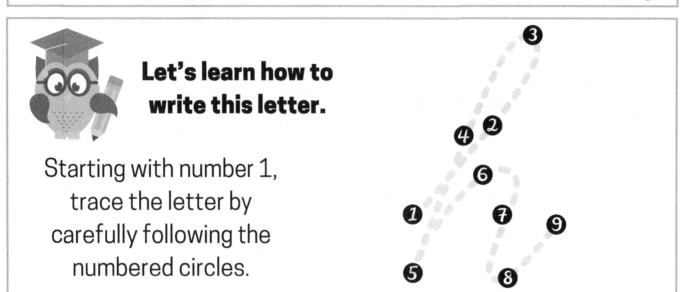

Starting with number 1, trace the letter by carefully following the numbered circles.

Now let's practice! Trace the letters using the example above.

h h h h h h h h

h h h h h h h h

h h h h h h h h

Your turn! Write the letter on your own.

h

$\mathcal{A}\ \mathcal{B}\ \mathcal{C}\ \mathcal{D}\ \mathcal{E}\ \mathcal{F}\ \mathcal{G}\ \mathcal{H}\ \mathcal{I}\ \mathcal{J}\ \mathcal{K}\ \mathcal{L}\ \mathcal{M}\ \mathcal{N}\ \mathcal{O}\ \mathcal{P}\ \mathcal{Q}\ \mathcal{R}\ \mathcal{S}\ \mathcal{T}\ \mathcal{U}\ \mathcal{V}\ \mathcal{W}\ \mathcal{X}\ \mathcal{Y}\ \mathcal{Z}$

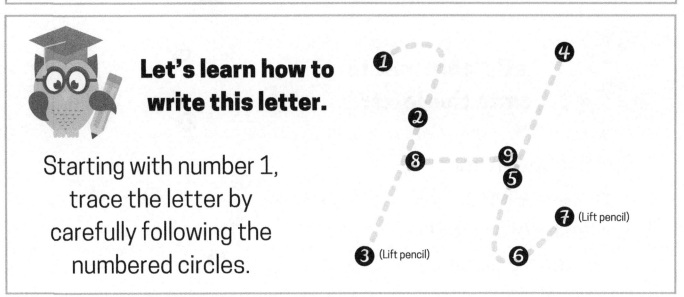

Let's learn how to write this letter.

Starting with number 1, trace the letter by carefully following the numbered circles.

Now let's practice! Trace the letters using the example above.

Your turn! Write the letter on your own.

a b c d e f g h **i** j k l m n o p q r s t u v w x y z

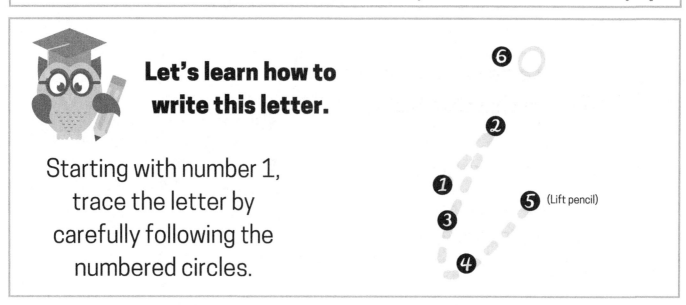

Let's learn how to write this letter.

Starting with number 1, trace the letter by carefully following the numbered circles.

⑥

②

① ⑤ (Lift pencil)

③

④

Now let's practice! Trace the letters using the example above.

Your turn! Write the letter on your own.

i

$ABCDEFGHIJKLMNOPQRSTUVWXYZ$

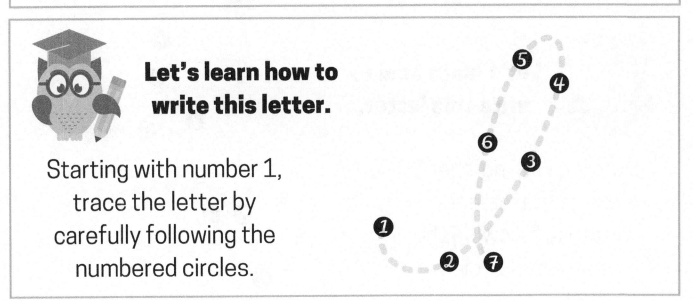

Let's learn how to write this letter.

Starting with number 1, trace the letter by carefully following the numbered circles.

Now let's practice! Trace the letters using the example above.

Your turn! Write the letter on your own.

Let's learn how to write this letter.

Starting with number 1, trace the letter by carefully following the numbered circles.

❼

❷

❶ ❻ (Lift pencil)

❺ ❸

❹

Now let's practice! Trace the letters using the example above.

Your turn! Write the letter on your own.

j

A B C D E F G H I J K L M N O P Q R S T U V W X Y Z

Let's learn how to write this letter.

Starting with number 1, trace the letter by carefully following the numbered circles.

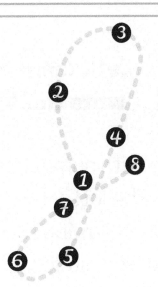

Now let's practice! Trace the letters using the example above.

Your turn! Write the letter on your own.

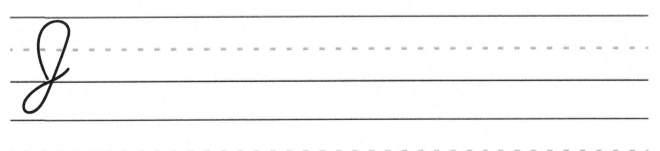

a b c d e f g h i j **k** *l m n o p q r s t u v w x y z*

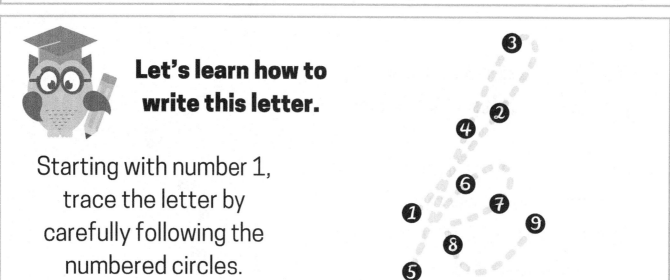

Let's learn how to write this letter.

Starting with number 1, trace the letter by carefully following the numbered circles.

Now let's practice! Trace the letters using the example above.

k k k k k k k k k k k k k k k k

k k k k k k k k k k k k k k k k

k k k k k k k k k k k k k k k k

Your turn! Write the letter on your own.

k

$\mathcal{A}\,\mathcal{B}\,\mathcal{C}\,\mathcal{D}\,\mathcal{E}\,\mathcal{F}\,\mathcal{G}\,\mathcal{H}\,\mathcal{I}\,\mathcal{J}$ K $\mathcal{L}\,\mathcal{M}\,\mathcal{N}\,\mathcal{O}\,\mathcal{P}\,\mathcal{Q}\,\mathcal{R}\,\mathcal{S}\,\mathcal{T}\,\mathcal{U}\,\mathcal{V}\,\mathcal{W}\,\mathcal{X}\,\mathcal{Y}\,\mathcal{Z}$

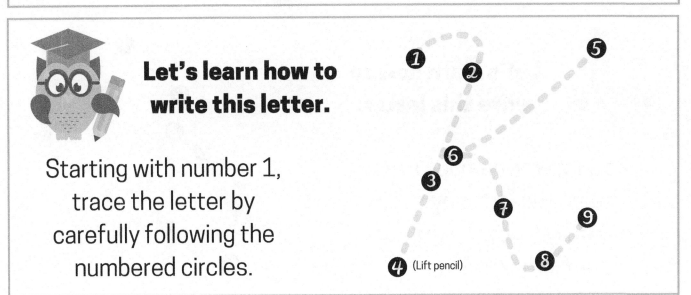

Let's learn how to write this letter.

Starting with number 1, trace the letter by carefully following the numbered circles.

(Lift pencil)

Now let's practice! Trace the letters using the example above.

Your turn! Write the letter on your own.

$\mathcal{K}$

a b c d e f g h i j k **l** *m n o p q r s t u v w x y z*

Let's learn how to write this letter.

Starting with number 1, trace the letter by carefully following the numbered circles.

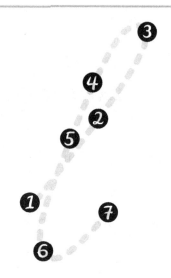

Now let's practice! Trace the letters using the example above.

Your turn! Write the letter on your own.

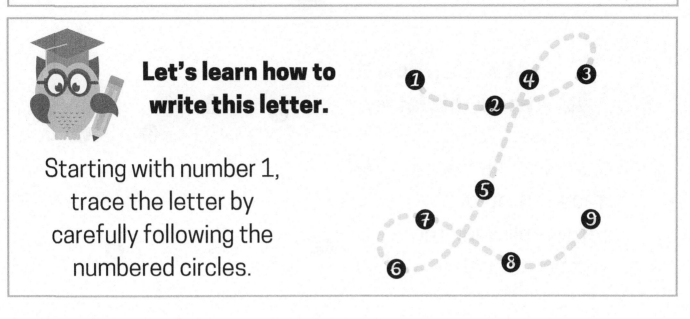

Let's learn how to write this letter.

Starting with number 1, trace the letter by carefully following the numbered circles.

Now let's practice! Trace the letters using the example above.

$\mathcal{L}$ $\mathcal{L}$ $\mathcal{L}$ $\mathcal{L}$ $\mathcal{L}$ $\mathcal{L}$ $\mathcal{L}$ $\mathcal{L}$ $\mathcal{L}$

$\mathcal{L}$ $\mathcal{L}$ $\mathcal{L}$ $\mathcal{L}$ $\mathcal{L}$ $\mathcal{L}$ $\mathcal{L}$ $\mathcal{L}$ $\mathcal{L}$

$\mathcal{L}$ $\mathcal{L}$ $\mathcal{L}$ $\mathcal{L}$ $\mathcal{L}$ $\mathcal{L}$ $\mathcal{L}$ $\mathcal{L}$ $\mathcal{L}$

Your turn! Write the letter on your own.

$\mathcal{L}$

Let's learn how to write this letter.

Starting with number 1, trace the letter by carefully following the numbered circles.

❶ ❷ ❸ ❹ ❺ ❻ ❼ ❽ ❾

Now let's practice! Trace the letters using the example above.

m m m m m m m m

m m m m m m m m

m m m m m m m m

Your turn! Write the letter on your own.

m

A B C D E F G H I J K L **M** N O P Q R S T U V W X Y Z

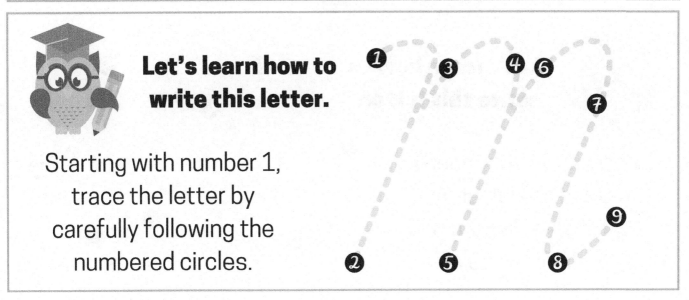

Let's learn how to write this letter.

Starting with number 1, trace the letter by carefully following the numbered circles.

Now let's practice! Trace the letters using the example above.

Your turn! Write the letter on your own.

M

a b c d e f g h i j k l m **n** o p q r s t u v w x y z

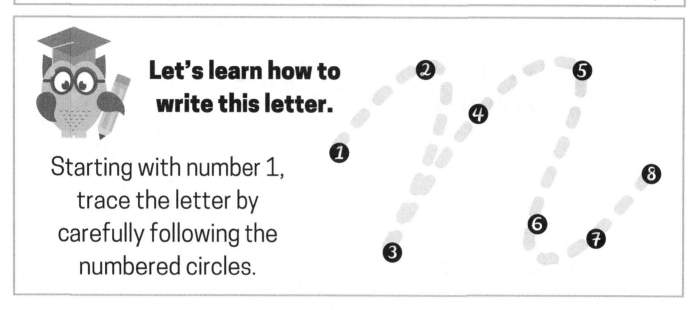

Let's learn how to write this letter.

Starting with number 1, trace the letter by carefully following the numbered circles.

Now let's practice! Trace the letters using the example above.

n n n n n n n n n n n n

n n n n n n n n n n n n

n n n n n n n n n n n n

Your turn! Write the letter on your own.

n

ABCDEFGHIJKLM**N**OPQRSTUVWXYZ

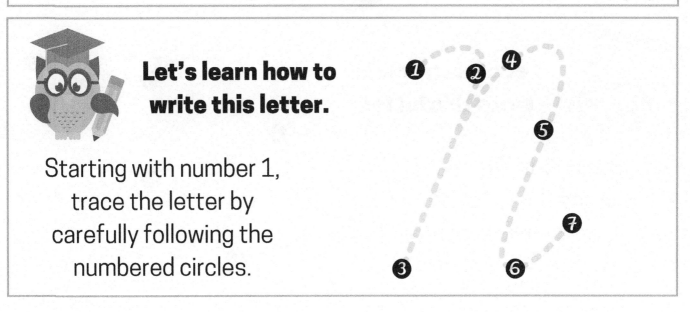

Let's learn how to write this letter.

Starting with number 1, trace the letter by carefully following the numbered circles.

Now let's practice! Trace the letters using the example above.

n n n n n n n n

n n n n n n n n

n n n n n n n n

Your turn! Write the letter on your own.

n

a b c d e f g h i j k l m n o p q r s t u v w x y z

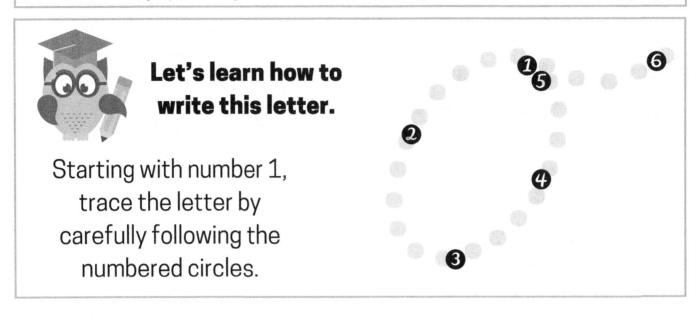

Let's learn how to write this letter.

Starting with number 1, trace the letter by carefully following the numbered circles.

Now let's practice! Trace the letters using the example above.

Your turn! Write the letter on your own.

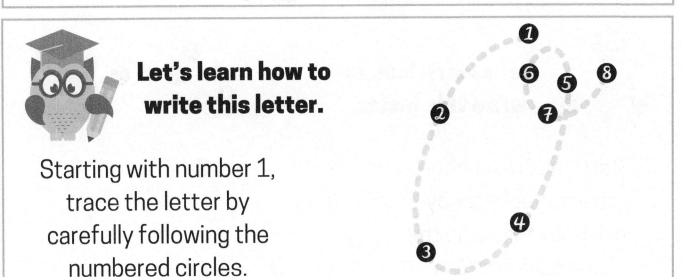

Let's learn how to write this letter.

Starting with number 1, trace the letter by carefully following the numbered circles.

Now let's practice! Trace the letters using the example above.

Your turn! Write the letter on your own.

a b c d e f g h i j k l m n o **p** q r s t u v w x y z

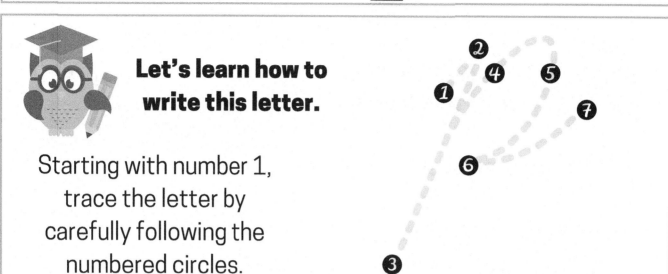

Let's learn how to write this letter.

Starting with number 1, trace the letter by carefully following the numbered circles.

Now let's practice! Trace the letters using the example above.

Your turn! Write the letter on your own.

p

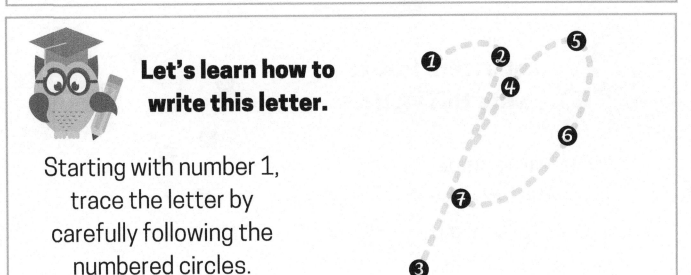

Let's learn how to write this letter.

Starting with number 1, trace the letter by carefully following the numbered circles.

Now let's practice! Trace the letters using the example above.

P P P P P P P P P P P

P P P P P P P P P P P

P P P P P P P P P P P

Your turn! Write the letter on your own.

P

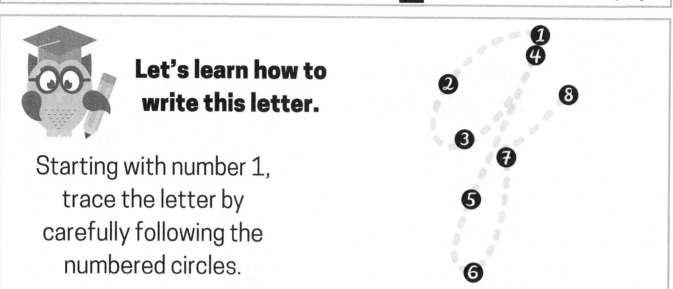

Starting with number 1, trace the letter by carefully following the numbered circles.

Now let's practice! Trace the letters using the example above.

Your turn! Write the letter on your own.

Let's learn how to write this letter.

Starting with number 1, trace the letter by carefully following the numbered circles.

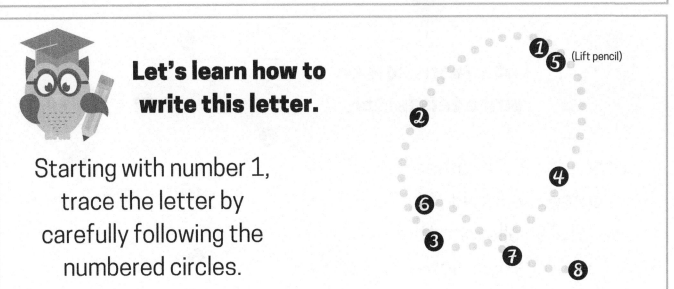

(Lift pencil)

Now let's practice! Trace the letters using the example above.

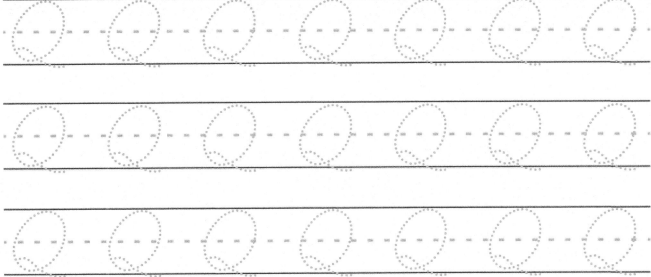

Your turn! Write the letter on your own.

$\mathcal{Q}$

Let's learn how to write this letter.

Starting with number 1, trace the letter by carefully following the numbered circles.

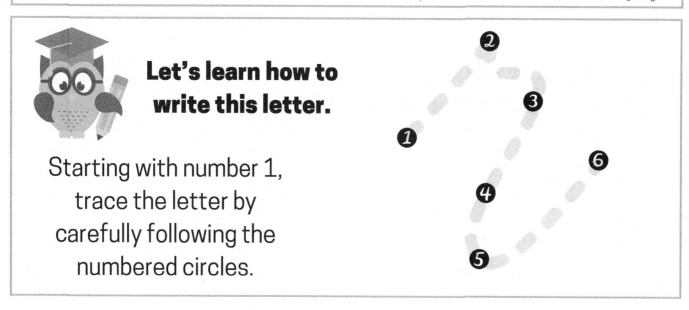

Now let's practice! Trace the letters using the example above.

Your turn! Write the letter on your own.

A B C D E F G H I J K L M N O P Q R S T U V W X Y Z

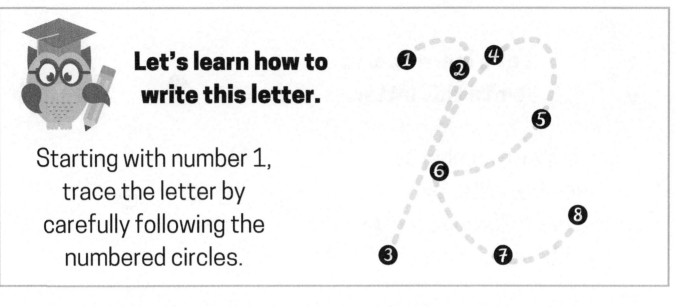

Let's learn how to write this letter.

Starting with number 1, trace the letter by carefully following the numbered circles.

Now let's practice! Trace the letters using the example above.

Your turn! Write the letter on your own.

R

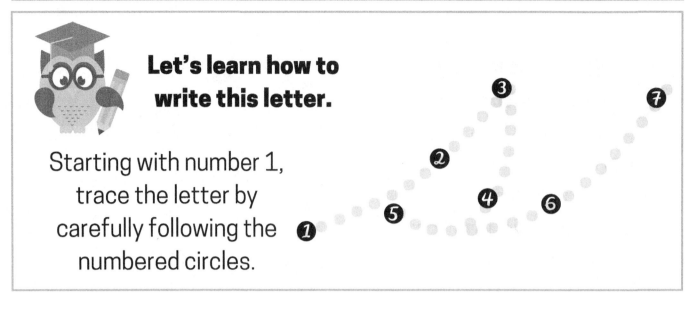

Let's learn how to write this letter.

Starting with number 1, trace the letter by carefully following the numbered circles.

Now let's practice! Trace the letters using the example above.

Your turn! Write the letter on your own.

Let's learn how to write this letter.

Starting with number 1, trace the letter by carefully following the numbered circles.

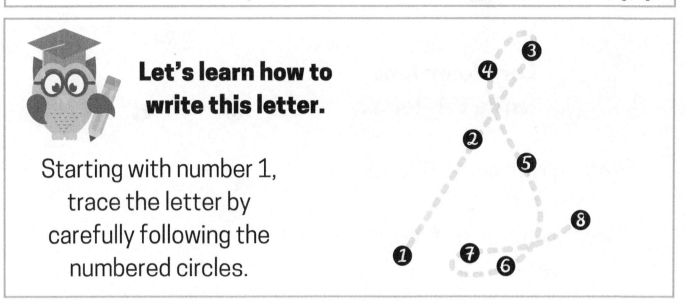

Now let's practice! Trace the letters using the example above.

Your turn! Write the letter on your own.

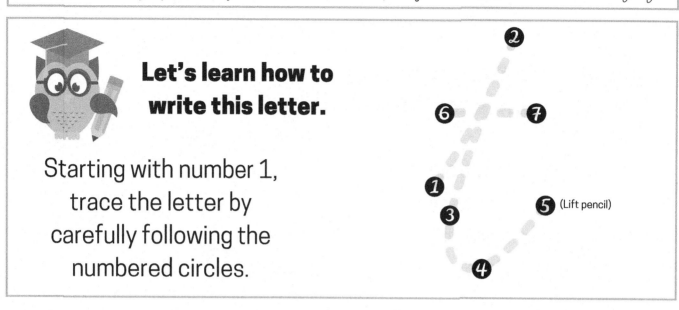

Starting with number 1, trace the letter by carefully following the numbered circles.

Now let's practice! Trace the letters using the example above.

t t t t t t t t t t

t t t t t t t t t t

t t t t t t t t t t

Your turn! Write the letter on your own.

t

$\mathcal{A}$ $\mathcal{B}$ $\mathcal{C}$ $\mathcal{D}$ $\mathcal{E}$ $\mathcal{F}$ $\mathcal{H}$ $\mathcal{I}$ $\mathcal{J}$ $\mathcal{K}$ $\mathcal{L}$ $\mathcal{M}$ $\mathcal{N}$ $\mathcal{O}$ $\mathcal{P}$ $\mathcal{Q}$ $\mathcal{R}$ $\mathcal{S}$ $\mathbf{\mathcal{T}}$ $\mathcal{U}$ $\mathcal{V}$ $\mathcal{W}$ $\mathcal{X}$ $\mathcal{Y}$ $\mathcal{Z}$

Let's learn how to write this letter.

Starting with number 1, trace the letter by carefully following the numbered circles.

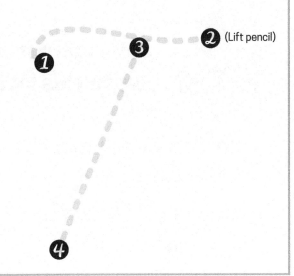

❶ ❸ ❷ (Lift pencil) ❹

Now let's practice! Trace the letters using the example above.

Your turn! Write the letter on your own.

a b c d e f g h i j k l m n o p q r s t **u** v w x y z

Let's learn how to write this letter.

Starting with number 1, trace the letter by carefully following the numbered circles.

❷ ❺

❶ ❼

❹

❸ ❻

Now let's practice! Trace the letters using the example above.

u u u u u u u u u u u

u u u u u u u u u u u

u u u u u u u u u u u

Your turn! Write the letter on your own.

U

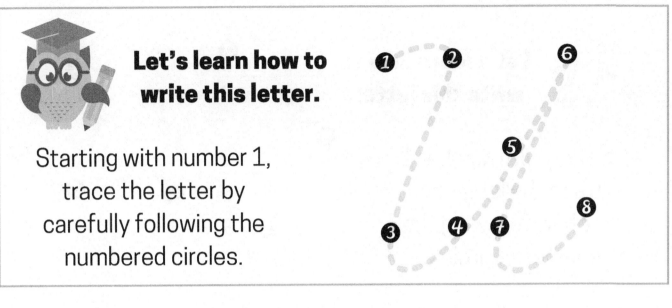

A B C D E F G H I J K L M N O P Q R S T **U** V W X Y Z

Let's learn how to write this letter.

Starting with number 1, trace the letter by carefully following the numbered circles.

Now let's practice! Trace the letters using the example above.

Your turn! Write the letter on your own.

$\mathcal{U}$

a b c d e f g h i j k l m n o p q r s t u **v** w x y z

Let's learn how to write this letter.

Starting with number 1, trace the letter by carefully following the numbered circles.

Now let's practice! Trace the letters using the example above.

Your turn! Write the letter on your own.

A B C D E F G H I J K L M N O P Q R S T U **V** *W X Y Z*

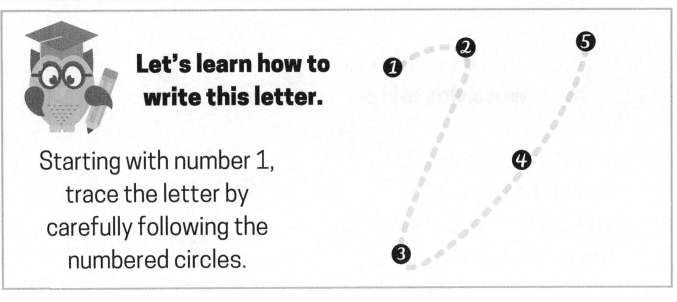

Let's learn how to write this letter.

Starting with number 1, trace the letter by carefully following the numbered circles.

Now let's practice! Trace the letters using the example above.

Your turn! Write the letter on your own.

a b c d e f g h i j k l m n o p q r s t u v **w** x y z

Let's learn how to write this letter.

Starting with number 1, trace the letter by carefully following the numbered circles.

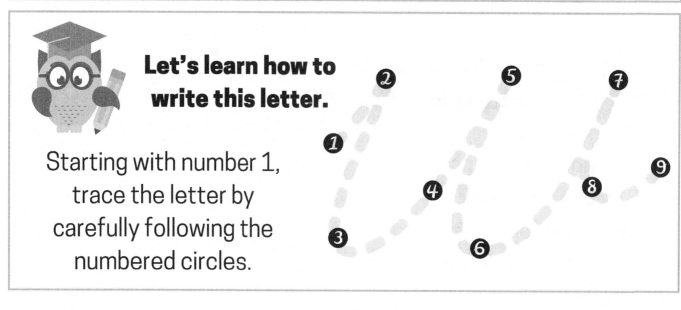

Now let's practice! Trace the letters using the example above.

Your turn! Write the letter on your own.

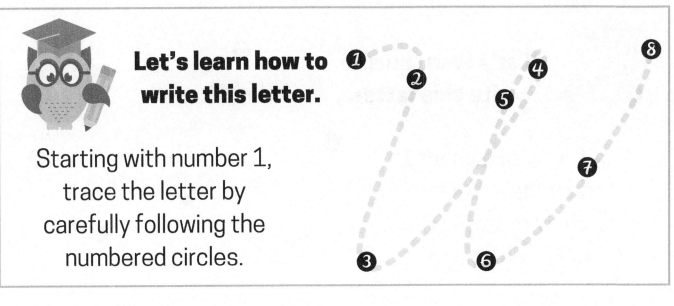

Let's learn how to write this letter.

Starting with number 1, trace the letter by carefully following the numbered circles.

Now let's practice! Trace the letters using the example above.

Your turn! Write the letter on your own.

a b c d e f g h i j k l m n o p q r s t u v w x y z

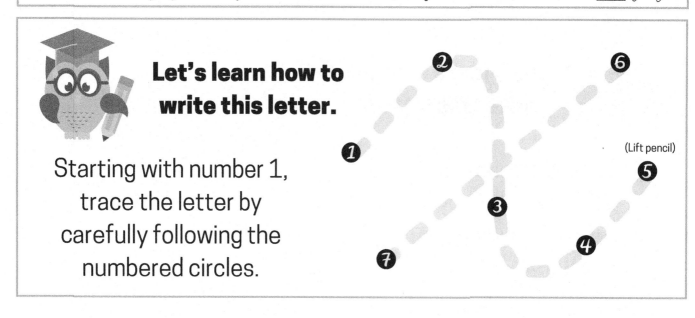

Let's learn how to write this letter.

Starting with number 1, trace the letter by carefully following the numbered circles.

(Lift pencil)

Now let's practice! Trace the letters using the example above.

Your turn! Write the letter on your own.

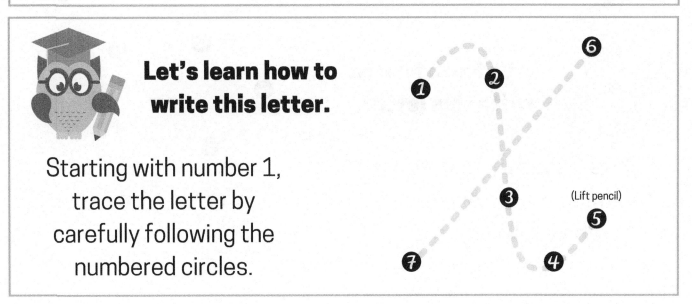

A B C D E F G H I J K L M N O P Q R S T U V W X Y Z

Let's learn how to write this letter.

Starting with number 1, trace the letter by carefully following the numbered circles.

(Lift pencil)

Now let's practice! Trace the letters using the example above.

Your turn! Write the letter on your own.

Let's learn how to write this letter.

Starting with number 1, trace the letter by carefully following the numbered circles.

① ❷ ❹ ❼ ❸ ❻ ❺

Now let's practice! Trace the letters using the example above.

Your turn! Write the letter on your own.

Y

Let's learn how to write this letter.

Starting with number 1, trace the letter by carefully following the numbered circles.

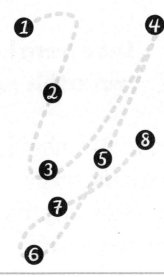

Now let's practice! Trace the letters using the example above.

Your turn! Write the letter on your own.

a b c d e f g h i j k l m n o p q r s t u v w x y **z**

Let's learn how to write this letter.

Starting with number 1, trace the letter by carefully following the numbered circles.

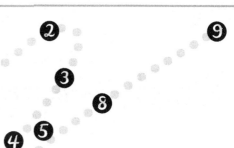

Now let's practice! Trace the letters using the example above.

Your turn! Write the letter on your own.

ABCDEFGHIJKLMNOPQRSTUVWXY

Let's learn how to write this letter.

Starting with number 1, trace the letter by carefully following the numbered circles.

❶ ❷ ❽ ❼ ❸ ❹ ❻ ❺

Now let's practice! Trace the letters using the example above.

Your turn! Write the letter on your own.

a b c d e f g h i j k l m n o p q r s t u v w x y z

A B C D E F G H I J K L M N O P Q R S T U V W X Y Z

 **Use this page to practice any letters that you found difficult.**

a b c d e f g h i j k l m n o p q r s t u v w x y z

A B C D E F G H I J K L M N O P Q R S T U V W X Y Z

 **Use this page to practice any letters that you found difficult.**

a b c d e f g h i j k l m n o p q r s t u v w x y z

A B C D E F G H I J K L M N O P Q R S T U V W X Y Z

Use this page to practice any letters that you found difficult.

Part 2: Connecting Letters

Here we join two letters together.
Follow the number guides to trace both letters and see how they are linked to each other.

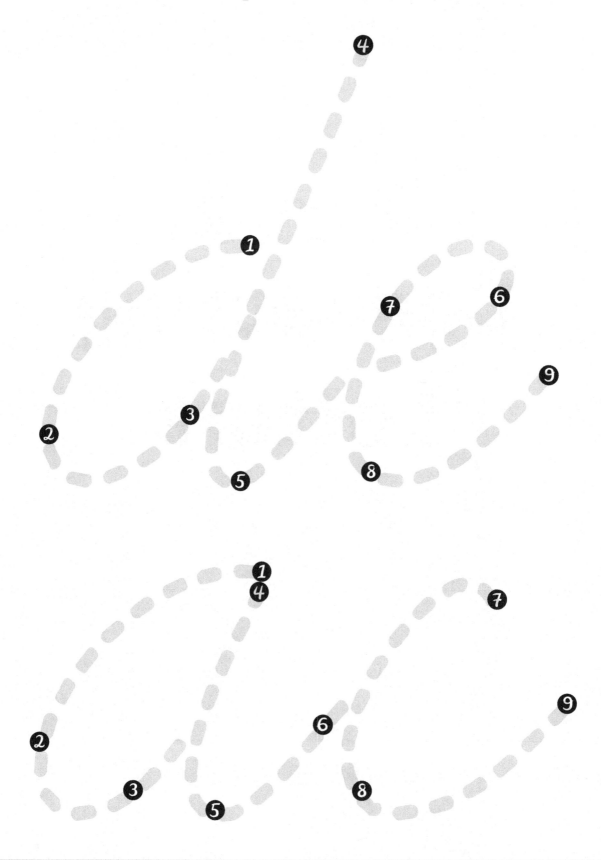

Let's look at a few more examples of linking letters.

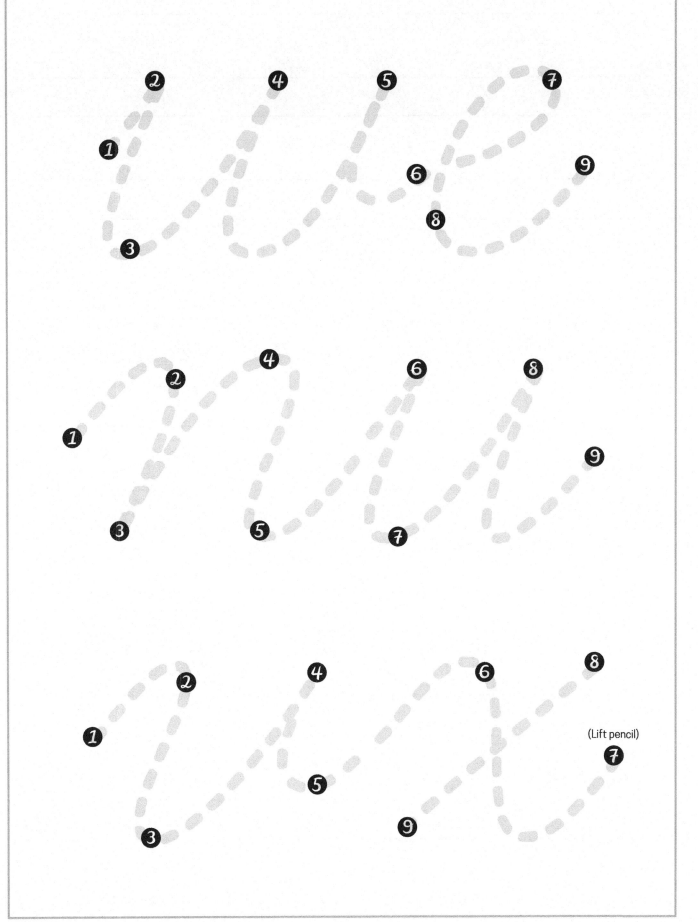

(Lift pencil)

Now you try! Trace the connected letters then try on your own

ge ge ge ge ge ge ge ge

ge

tl tl tl tl tl tl tl tl tl

tl

uu uu uu uu uu

uu

Trace the connected letters then try on your own

yc yc yc yc yc yc yc

yc

ju ju ju ju ju ju ju

ju

cc cc cc cc cc cc cc cc

cc

Trace the connected letters then try on your own

ma ma ma ma ma

ma

dp dp dp dp dp dp

dp

bi bi bi bi bi bi bi bi

bi

Trace the connected letters then try on your own

gg gg gg gg gg gg gg

gg

fk fk fk fk fk fk fk

fk

hn hn hn hn hn hn

hn

Trace the connected letters then try on your own

qr qr qr qr qr qr qr

qr

xy xy xy xy xy xy

xy

tr tr tr tr tr tr tr

tr

Trace the connected letters then try on your own

He He He He He He

He

Ja Ja Ja Ja Ja Ja

Ja

Kc Kc Kc Kc Kc Kc

Kc

Trace the connected letters then try on your own

Lp Lp Lp Lp Lp

Lp

Yb Yb Yb Yb Yb Yb

Yb

Cc Cc Cc Cc Cc Cc Cc

Cc

Trace the connected letters then try on your own

Uk Uk Uk Uk Uk

Uk

Ri Ri Ri Ri Ri Ri

Ri

Gg Gg Gg Gg Gg

Gg

Trace the connected letters then try on your own

Uu Uu Uu Uu Uu

Uu

Pi Pi Pi Pi Pi Pi Pi Pi

Pi

Ee Ee Ee Ee Ee Ee Ee Ee

Ee

Part 3: Writing Words

(They start easy, but get harder!)

baby baby baby baby

Trace the word then copy it in the space beneath.

girl girl girl girl girl

glad glad glad glad

Trace the word then copy it in the space beneath.

hand hand hand

truck   truck   truck

Trace the word then copy it in the space beneath.

name   name   name

late late late late late

Trace the word then copy it in the space beneath.

wind wind wind

nice *nice* *nice* *nice*

Trace the word then copy it in the space beneath.

candy *candy* *candy*

lunch   lunch   lunch

Trace the word then copy it in the space beneath.

away   away   away

club club club club

Trace the word then copy it in the space beneath.

what what what

drive *drive* *drive*

Trace the word then copy it in the space beneath.

very very very very

each each each each

Trace the word then copy it in the space beneath.

tree tree tree tree tree

farm *farm* *farm*

Trace the word then copy it in the space beneath.

riding *riding* *riding*

cattle *cattle* *cattle*

Trace the word then copy it in the space beneath.

dinner dinner dinner

heard heard heard

Trace the word then copy it in the space beneath.

family family family

inches   inches   inches

Trace the word then copy it in the space beneath.

Juice   Juice   Juice

Kitten Kitten Kitten

Trace the word then copy it in the space beneath.

Large Large Large

Merry Merry Merry

Trace the word then copy it in the space beneath.

Picture Picture Picture

Shield Shield Shield

Trace the word then copy it in the space beneath.

Running Running

Under Under Under

Trace the word then copy it in the space beneath.

Value Value Value

Winter Winter Winter

Trace the word then copy it in the space beneath.

Xray Xray Xray

remember remember

Trace the word then copy it in the space beneath.

yesterday yesterday

Different   Different

Trace the word then copy it in the space beneath.

Suddenly   Suddenly

President   *President*

Trace the word then copy it in the space beneath.

Sentence   *Sentence*

happiness happiness

Trace the word then copy it in the space beneath.

Beautiful Beautiful

medicine medicine

Trace the word then copy it in the space beneath.

maximum maximum

I am great at writing

Trace the word then copy it in the space beneath.

I deserve a treat

Practice Paper

Go over any words that you found difficult and try to write your own words

Made in the USA
Monee, IL
14 January 2022

88957262R00059